Smiles from Schooldays

John Hobson

Published by

MELROSE BOOKS

An Imprint of Melrose Press Limited
St Thomas Place, Ely
Cambridgeshire
CB7 4GG, UK
www.melrosebooks.co.uk

FIRST EDITION

Copyright © John Hobson 2017

The Author asserts his moral right to
be identified as the author of this work

Cover by Melrose Books

ISBN 978-1-912026-16-6
epub 978-1-912026-17-3
mobi 978-1-912026-18-0

Printed and bound in Great Britain by:
Airdrie Print Services Ltd
24-26 Flowerhill Street
Airdrie, North Lanarkshire
Scotland, ML6 6BH

I dedicate my book to our elder son,
Sherren John Hobson.
He encouraged me in this project,
supplied elusive words in the English Language
section, but succumbed to cancer
in October 2016.

Acknowledgement

I have relied on my grandson, Daniel, for aspects of the interaction with the publishers, Melrose Books, requiring computer expertise.

Contents

Physics

❖ Mrs. Newton, known for her
  unqualified devotion,
  would run and jump and skip to prove
  Sir Isaac's laws of motion.

Physics

❖ Mrs. Newton's problem was
too much for her to grapple.
"How can Isaac's law be based
on one ripe falling apple?"

Physics

❖ Mrs. Archimedes was
surprised to hear a streaker
rushing from the bathroom yell,
"DISPLACEMENT! OH, EUREKA!"

Physics

❖ Electric motors didn't puzzle
Mrs. Faraday,
as long as Michael's magnetism
didn't go away.

❖ Is there any pleasure,
or even satisfaction,
in knowing every action
has an opposite reaction?

❖ Mrs. Einstein, keen to show
her creativity,
would illustrate old Albert's laws
of relativity.

❖ 12 years in space
for 500 million miles,
Rosetta probe control
certainly saw some scientific smiles.

Physics

❖ One's energetic output
   need never be impaired
   by not entirely knowing why
   $E=mc^2$.

Physics

❖ Energy can be produced
  from many a natural source;
  waterfalls, volcanic steam,
  the tides and wind of course.
  Another with potential
  to outdo them all by miles
  is the mc^2 created
  by renewing people's smiles.

❖ If the man-in-the-moon's ill-mannered,
  or merely misbehaves,
  no doubt they'll find the reason
  through gravitational waves.

Biology

❖ Mrs. Darwin never went
to far Galapagos:
She wondered, "Could a slug evolve
into an albatross?"

Biology

❖ Pre-war, in our little village school
   with its blackboard and its chalk,
   we were glad when teacher said,
   "It's fine, let's have a nature walk."

❖ Chlorophyl produces
   all the lovely shades of green
   beloved by teenage wood-nymphs
   since they were sweet sixteen.

❖ Photosynthesis creates
   a lot of nice fresh air,
   especially at the seaside
   like Weston-super-Mare.

Biology

❖ Many birdsongs make you think
what a lovely way to talk,
but not the thieving magpie's
very unattractive squawk.

❖ Contemplating origins,
one probable solution
remains the one that Charles proposed
concerning evolution.

❖ To monitor my blood, I went
to the phlebotomist
and when she stuck the needle in
she very rarely missed.

Chemistry

❖ Mr. Curie kept quite fit
   by jogging round the stadium
   while his wife was labouring in the lab
   in patient search of radium.

❖ Looking back, he still has trouble
   sorting fact from fable,
   never having understood
   the periodic table.

❖ If Democritus was cheerful,
   he had good cause to be.
   He shared his thoughts on atoms
   democritic'ly.

❖ Never mind if you're a lad
   or whether you're a lass,
   you're going to have to learn
   what constitutes a noble gas.

Psychology

❖ Mrs. Pavlov wondered
why the dinner bell was ringing
and why her husband Ivan
so quickly started singing
in great delight when his three dogs
started salivating
at lots of lovely liver
they'd been anticipating.

Psychology

❖ The disappointed flirt became
 a little bit annoyed
 when told her psychoanalyst
 would not be Sigmund Freud.

❖ Mr. Maslow's hierarchy
 of basic human needs
 excludes such brassy baubles
 as bangles, bells and beads.

❖ Mrs. Freud is quite concerned
 and more so than it seems
 when Sigmund finds the way
 to psychoanalyse her dreams.

Maths

❖ Mrs. Pythagoras wondered why
  it made the evening news
  that two old squares could equal one
  on the hypotenuse.

13

Maths

❖ Mrs. Einstein knew no maths
  beyond, say, two times two.
  She didn't know what people meant
  by Albert's high I.Q.

Maths

❖ Mrs. Newton said she liked
  a minus more than plus
  but didn't have a clue
  what Isaac meant by calculus.

❖ Denominators see a lot
  of rather common action
  especially when confronted
  by a very vulgar fraction.

Maths

❖ Mrs. Euclid's grasp of maths
  was rather incomplete.
  She wasn't sure why she should care
  that train lines never meet.

Maths

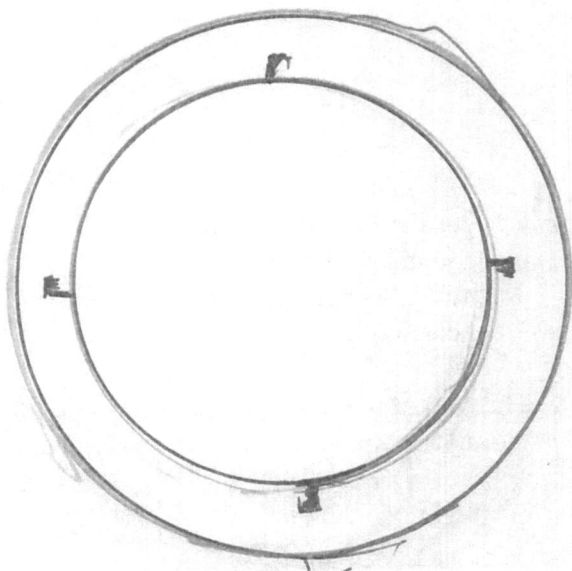

❖ The matador knew no expense
  had been foreseen or spared
  in building Ronda's bullring,
  a mighty πr^2.

Maths

❖ The cat slept in the corner,
  content and softly purring,
  dreaming, "Is a nice round π,
  3.1 recurring?"

❖ The sum of a triangle's angles
  throughout the seven seas
  will never be precisely
  one eight one degrees.

History

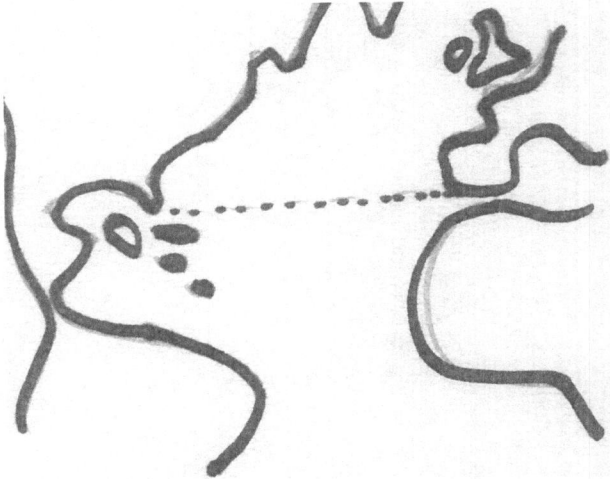

❖ Mrs. Columbus stayed at home
while Chris was off exploring.
Though pleased to find America,
he found the crossing boring.

History

❖ Cleopatra never married,
  that was her mistake.
  Better to embrace a man
  than some short, slimy snake.

History

❖ The need for wearing wellingtons,
   (a prudent thing to do),
   arises, so they say,
   from a muddy, watery loo.

❖ Was King Canute a married man?
   Was there a blushing bride?
   Did she go down the beach with him
   to try to turn the tide?

History

❖ Mrs. Ford thought Henry faced
  considerable flak
  when his model T's rolled off the line
  but only came in black.

History

❖ Mrs. Galileo said,
   "When all is said and done,
   I support my husband's claim,
   we're whizzing round the sun.
   This doesn't please the Catholics,
   it upsets their position,
   so we shall very soon appear
   before the inquisition."

❖ Suggesting Mrs. Fawkes'
   participation in the plot,
   old Guy was disappointed
   when she said, "I'd rather not."

❖ Mrs. Hillary heard the news
   while helping with the fencing
   that Edmund H had reached the top
   with his loyal Sherpa Tensing.

History

❖ Lady Drake, surprisingly,
   achieved some modest goals
   of which the most remarkable,
   she beat Sir Frank at bowls!

History

❖ Mrs. Nixon won't forget
the inauspicious date
when tricky Dicky rued the day
he went to Watergate.

❖ Mrs. Tyler was subdued
when in her husband's presence.
She'd heard that Wat and his few friends
were all revolting peasants.

❖ Mrs. Lincoln was upset when,
sitting in her seat,
someone fired a gun at Abe,
a most unpleasant feat.

History

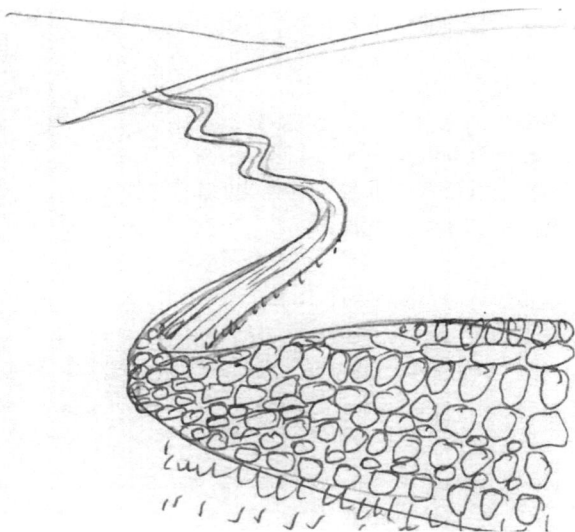

❖ Mrs. Hadrian helped her husband
  build his winding wall
  but it didn't keep the Scottish out
  of England after all.

History

❖ Mrs. Fleming did the garden,
   tendin' and a-tillin'
   while Alexander stayed indoors
   discovering penicillin.

❖ Runnymede's a pleasant place
   where barons once had gone
   to introduce a great big charter,
   sealed by bad King John.

❖ Lady Nelson's discontent
   was just a little tardy.
   Horatio'd already said,
   "Please kiss me, Mr. Hardy."

History

❖ Mrs. Tell was horrified
on seeing Will take aim.
If he should miss and hit their son
it would be such a shame.

History

❖ Elizabeth the First decided to
  usurp her sister and
  resisted the advances of
  each potential mister.

❖ Mrs. Ghandi realised
  in 1933
  how difficult their life would be
  democratic'ly.

❖ Mrs. Nero met her husband
  in the local choir.
  She showed him how to execute
  and light a Roman fire.

History

❖ Mrs. Turpin fed the horses,
  Dandelion and Dobbin.
  As soon as Dick returned at night
  from his routine highway robbin'

History

❖ Al Capone, a married man,
  in 1936,
  told his wife that prohibition
  wasn't hard to fix.

❖ Mrs. Wisdom always said,
  "The best of dear old Norman
  was when he fell that second time
  and tripped the storeman foreman."

❖ Mrs. Confucius was around
  when reasoning began,
  and her husband said, with Chinese
  wisdom, "Love your fellow man."

History

❖ Nero's mother met her end
   at his capricious hand
   in '64, with Rome in flames,
   he played to beat the band.

❖ Henry Five, a bachelor,
   fancied the French princess
   so after the "do" at Agincourt
   and his famous loud address,
   he wondered how to plight his troth
   and figure what to say
   to win another victory
   AFTER St Crispin's Day.

History

❖ Bonaparte became
   a little better than he'd been
   before his stock dropped in the eyes
   of Empress Josephine.

❖ Charles II liked to think
   he was devoid of sin
   until he found a lady-friend
   called Nell (of the House of Gwynn).

❖ Marie Antoinette still liked
   her cake as much as bread
   until in 1793
   she lost her silly head.

History

❖ Everyone knows 1066
   was when the Normans landed,
   but no-one knew the bowman
   who shot Harold was left-handed!

History

❖ Mrs. Caxton lit the fire
each day in deep midwinter
to keep Bill warm as he worked hard
to be a perfect printer.

❖ Mrs. Genghis, as a Mongol,
bore a future Mongol Khan
who conquered Chinese neighbours
along their unpaved autobahn.

❖ Romulus had Remus
as his closest kin at home.
After their wolf-nourishment,
he found a place called Rome.

Geography

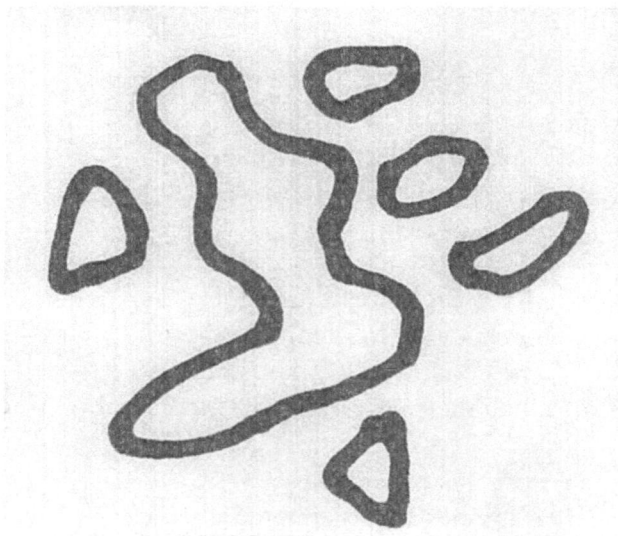

❖ Mrs. Darwin, bless her,
  was somewhat at a loss
  when asked one day in Sainsbury's,
  "Where IS Galapagos?"

Geography

❖ Mrs. Livingstone stayed at home,
   not feeling very manly,
   while Mr. L toured Africa
   in search of Mr. Stanley.

❖ We cruised Norwegian fjords
   full of wonder and intrigue
   and walked the streets of Bergen
   in the steps of Edvard Greig.

❖ It has the shortest name of all
   as lengthy rivers go.
   Look at your atlas to discover,
   "Where's the mighty Po?"

Geography

❖ Sherpa Tensing was surprised
  when chasing a fritillary
  to find himself up Everest with
  the great Sir Edmund Hillary.

Geography

❖ Of the four oceans in the world,
   much bigger than I'd reckoned,
   Pacific's nearly twice as big
   as Atlantic (placing second).

❖ Philately may be a way,
   before you go to college,
   to brush-up on the details of
   your geographic knowledge.

Geography

❖ If Shangri-La is situated
high up in Tibet,
it's not surprising none of us
has ever found it yet.

Geography

❖ If every country's creatures
   were designed and made by God,
   then that first Friday afternoon
   The Grand Banks got their cod.

❖ Along the coast of Newfoundland
   the views are very nice,
   enhanced by watching great big whales
   and bigger bergs of ice.

❖ I understand you lost your way
   en route to fairyland.
   It's on the coast of the Avalon
   in eastern Newfoundland.

❖ The longest waterway in the world
   would take you quite a while
   to swim downstream to Cairo
   from the source of the River Nile.

Art

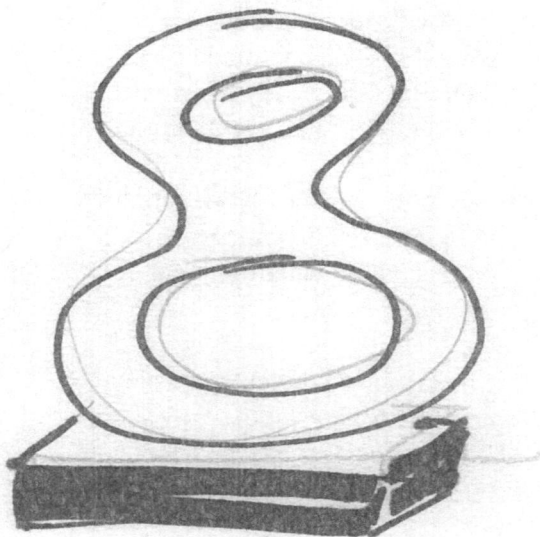

❖ Mrs. Moore played croquet games
  and sometimes even bowls
  while Henry spent his afternoons
  just carving concrete holes.

Art

❖ Mrs. Picasso sometimes wondered,
   "What's the big appeal
   of Pablo's cubic pictures,
   so quaint and so surreal."

❖ Mrs. Lowry's life in Salford
   changed forever when
   her husband started painting scenes
   with lots of matchstick men.

Art

❖ Mrs. Michelangelo
found her husband's work appealing
especially when he undertook
to paint the chapel ceiling.

Art

❖ Mrs. V. G. said it seemed
   exceptionally clear
   that Vincent's Sunflowers, actually,
   would not be worth his ear.

❖ Mrs. Da Vinci leaned against
   the famous tower in Pisa
   when Leonardo told her he
   had drawn the Mona Lisa.

❖ Mrs. Manet promised Eddie
   she would raise a glass
   to his success in painting
   that rude picnic on the grass.

Art

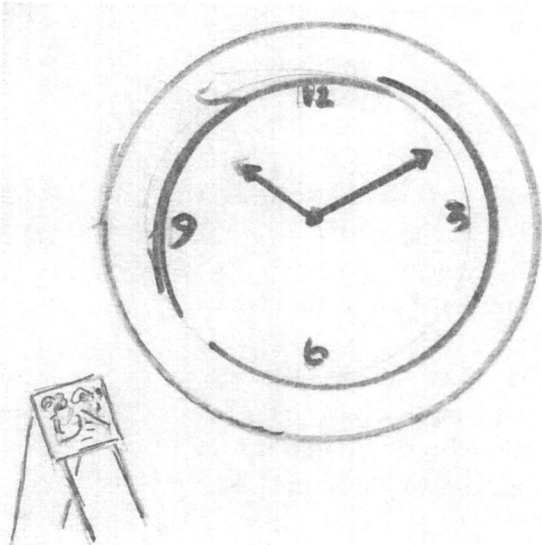

❖ Mrs. Constable wondered where
her kitchen clock had gone
until she found, eventually,
her famous husband, John,
was guilty of removing it.
He never seemed to cease
from measuring the time it takes
to paint a masterpiece.

Art

❖ Mrs. Da Vinci, I suppose,
   played her domestic part
   by seeing that Leonardo
   got fed before his art.

❖ Mrs. Caravaggio
   exclaimed, "It isn't right,
   my son has had to flee from Rome
   for being in a fight!"

❖ Mrs. Dali couldn't cook,
   her painting too was poor
   so she left the money-making jobs
   to hubby, Salvador.

Art

❖ Mrs. Gaugin's son decided,
   feeling somewhat "fleety",
   he had had enough of France
   so he took off for Tahiti.

❖ Mrs. Rodin realised
   her cheeks were glowing pinker
   when Auguste finished sculpting both
   The Kiss and then The Thinker.

❖ Mrs. Constable walked along
   a Suffolk country lane
   and came across her husband
   painting hay inside a wain.

Art

❖ Mrs. Monet soon became
more tolerant and fond
of Claude when he came home to paint
their water lily pond.

❖ When David emerged from the marble block,
so tall and so sublime,
Michelangelo knew that he
was in there all the time.

❖ Caravaggio's character
may sometimes dismay us
but nonetheless we do
admire his "Supper in Emmaus"

Music

❖ Mrs. Mozart knew his manners
   bordered on atrocious,
   Amadeus having been
   a child somewhat precocious.

❖ Mrs. Burns thought Robert was
   imbibing too much wine
   but he's remembered ev'ry time
   we sing of auld lang syne.

❖ All the kin of young Saint-Saëns
   were proud of his success
   and so were all the animals
   at the Carnival, no less.

Music

❖ Mrs. Waller gave her full
   affection to her cats
   who kept on misbehavin'
   and irritatin' Fats.

❖ Mrs. Bunyan travelled
   all the way to County Antrim
   valiantly convincing John
   she'd try to be a pilgrim.

❖ Mrs. Schubert's love of music
   was quite undiminished,
   knowing her husband's symphony
   was famously unfinished.

Music

❖ Mrs. Holst taught Gus to read
  with tales of Johns and Janets.
  When he grew up he much preferred
  to write about the planets.

❖ When Andre Previn played some Grieg,
  I was an applauder
  for he struck the notes, unlike Eric,
  in just the proper order.

❖ Mrs. Blake shared William's hope
  the time would surely come
  when we would build in Warwickshire
  a new Jerusalem.

Music

❖ Mrs. Paganini cried,
  for strange as it may seem,
  she loved the variation on
  Niccolò's well-known theme.

❖ Mrs. Gershwin donned a dress
  of such a sky-like hue
  that George declared his wife became
  a rhapsody in blue.

❖ Mrs. Elgar realised
  without a touch of malice
  that Edward needed company
  from a much younger Alice.

Music

❖ J.S.Bach, undoubtedly
a most accomplished fellow,
but could he play his six suites on
his charismatic cello?

❖ We'd like to go with all the Harrys,
Dicks and all the Toms
each early in September
to the Last Night of the Proms.

❖ Before each International,
they play the Anthem first.
I'm quite relieved when we don't have
to sing the second verse.

Music

❖ Mrs. Wagner thought (like Twain,
  who did the comic rounds),
  Richard's Götterdämmerung
  is better than it sounds.

❖ Miss Coppélia danced her way
  through fantasy and folly,
  forgetting she was nothing but
  a dual-duty dolly.

❖ Whoever were his next of kin,
  what most of us admire,
  is Handel's oratorio,
  the marvellous *Messiah*.

Music

❖ Mrs. Bach would not have lived
 on much restricted rations
 once J.S. had done composing
 several of his passions.

❖ The lyrics to Prokofiev's
 patriotic score
 inspire a rather gory call
 to a very bloody war.

❖ No concerto is so sweet
 and none considered finer
 than Elgar's for the cello
 in Edward's old E minor.

Music

❖ When the Gershwin brothers wrote
   their light, romantic songs,
   Ira had to figure out
   where every word belongs.

❖ Mrs. Rachmanonov said that she
   had never even heard
   of a piano concerto quite as long
   as her good husband's 3rd.

❖ Wagner (at the Albert Hall),
   the Proms most played performer,
   undoubtedly disturbs, I'm sure,
   the most determined dozer.

R.E.

❖ David's daddy must have taught him
how to use a sling.
He hit Goliath with a stone
which hurt like anything.

R.E.

❖ To be admitted, you don't have
   to wait until invited.
   Just tell St. Peter you're a fan
   of Manchester United.

❖ Adam and Eve had five young kids
   around the kitchen table.
   They fed them lots of fish and chips,
   especially Cain and Abel.

❖ Mrs. Lot thought she had got
   a man without a fault
   until her careless looking-back
   produced a heap of salt.

R.E.

❖ Delilah was a lady who
now and then confides
she gave Samson a haircut,
shortish back and sides.

R.E.

❖ We're not told if Jonah had
a wife in that old tale
of when he took his morning dip
and swam into a whale.

❖ Someone must have counted Judas
in their family tree
but with his reputation –
quite reluctantly.

❖ They couldn't quite believe their luck,
those young men, by 'n by,
when they received permission to
go forth and multiply.

R.E.

❖ Jacob's mum would hardly have
  been more upset or sadder
  if he had missed his footing and
  fallen off the ladder.

R.E.

❖ Moses' mother might have been
   a little broken hearted
   if on the day they ran away,
   the water hadn't parted.

❖ St. Peter's friend, a fisherman
   with a very pretty daughter,
   could hardly quite believe he saw
   a person walk on water.

❖ Ruth showed her devotion by
   performing all the cleaning
   for Naomi and her household
   when she wasn't busy gleaning.

R.E.

❖ Eve's a famous lady
with very little on
who wanders through the orchard
where Adam Smith had gone.
She doesn't pick a Bramley
(her cooking is a pain),
her pref'rence is an 'eater',
a Worcestershire Pearmain.

R.E.

❖ Articulating doggedly
   as well as they were able,
   they found it very difficult
   inside the Tower of Babel.

❖ Having so many sons to raise,
   their mum had one last dote;
   at the local M&S bought Joe
   a multi-coloured coat.

❖ When Saul and his relations had
   that well-known roadside fright
   Damascus-bound, he must have said,
   "Good Lord, I've seen the light!"

R.E.

❖ Joshua's missus joined the shout
on the last lap round the city
but said, when Jericho collapsed,
"Oh Moses! What a pity!"

R.E.

❖ The mothers in the multitude
  with babies on their hips
  were quite surprised when they received
  so many fish & chips.

❖ Standing at The Gate all day,
  sorting saints from sinners,
  Peter has his work cut out
  deciding on the winners.

❖ When Eve was in the Garden,
  was she looking rather glum
  at finding she had picked
  a rotten apple with aplomb?

❖ If cleanliness is Godliness
  as those who know it say,
  we'd better take a thorough shower
  a dozen times a day.

P.E.

_____

❖ The object of a rugby game,
   if you were wondering why
   they struggle in the wind and rain,
   is to score a simple try.

P.E.

❖ If you ever wondered what
   is meant by "it's a sticky wicket"
   and "silly point" and "one short leg",
   it's the mystery of cricket.

❖ Nadia Comenici became
   gymnastic champion when,
   at Montreal in '76,
   she scored a perfect 10.

❖ What tumblers do these days, I think,
   is utterly fantastic!
   Their somersaults on beam and bars
   are dangerously gymnastic.

P.E.

❖ Regular this and regular that,
  the old folks may advise,
  but the best advice that grandma gives
  is regular exercise.

P.E.

❖ When Don was stuck on 99,
  Mrs. Bradman wondered
  why he'd want to get another
  faultless flippin' hundred.

❖ The pole-vault disregards the laws
  of gravity and thus
  propels the best performers
  over a London Bus.

❖ To reach Olympic standard calls
  for so much dedication,
  is winning gold or even bronze
  sufficient just'fication?

P.E.

❖ Can you believe some men can jump
   amazingly as high
   as the ceiling in your living room?
   No? Neither, sir, can I.

❖ I like a game where everyone
   is active all the time,
   not sitting down and waiting for
   their turn till half-past nine.

❖ Looking for a long life
   and keeping fairly fit?
   Silly short leg fielding
   is certainly not it.

❖ Exercising brawn and brain,
   frying bacon in the rain,
   tested her ability
   doing the silver D. of E.

Philosophy

❖ Mrs. Plato, with a sigh,
  decided, "It's ironic,
  our rather long relationship
  is really quite platonic."

❖ One wonders whether anyone,
  preferring time alone,
  can live a life of solitude
  on a minute mobile phone.

❖ Mrs. Keynes was pleased to hear
  her husband favoured spending.
  She spent more time in Oxford Street
  than he had been intending.

Philosophy

❖ Ancient Athens wondered how
to mind their qs and ps.
The man who would philosophise,
of course, was Socrates.

❖ *Critique of Reason* is a book
most certainly extant,
a very good example
of what is known as Kant.

❖ Mrs. Aristophanes knew
just what husbands liked
and her husband knew it too, of course,
when he wrote of the women's strike.

Philosophy

- ❖ archy and mehitabel,
  examples of the notion
  that someone's soul can relocate
  despite Ike's laws of motion.

- ❖ If Einstein had been subject to
  a period in captivity,
  would it have affected
  his thoughts on relativity?

- ❖ Christmas time's exciting
  for the children who may pause
  to wonder whether, way up north,
  there's a Mrs. Santa Claus.

Philosophy

❖ "The daddy of geometry"
   is what they called Descartes.
   Famous French philosopher,
   he had a hefty heart.

❖ One wonders what to make of it
   if "life is but a dream".
   Philosophers who said it may
   be wiser than they seem …

❖ Copernicus concluded
   that the earth goes round the sun.
   Like Ptolemy before him,
   he ptaught most anyone.

❖ The power of positive thinking
   and an optimistic air
   may just prolong your life-time
   and cut the cost of care.

Mythology

❖ Icarus took off one day,
 free flying just for fun.
 He felt quite hot and, just too late,
 heard Dad yell, "MIND THE SUN!"

Mythology

❖ Midas had a mother,
   she wasn't very old,
   I bet she hoped her little boy
   would be as good as gold.

❖ Aphrodite had no kin
   as far as I can tell
   but, Goddess of Fertility,
   she compensated well.

❖ Achilles' mummy popped him,
   as a baby, in the Styx
   but dangling him by his little heel
   she left him in a fix.

Mythology

❖ Echo didn't fancy Pan,
   she much preferred Narcissus.
   She lost 'em both and ended up
   as no-one's little missus.

❖ Jason was an Argonaut
   whose well-known party-piece
   was playing hunt the thimble
   but he really sought some fleece.

❖ Mrs. Pendragon nurtured Arthur
   much as she was able
   until he branched out on his own
   and found a nice round table.

Mythology

❖ The Mediterranean Sea has borne
the very high and mighty
but none as slim and beautiful
as the naked Aphrodite.

❖ Poseidon's brother Zeus said,
"Let's make an earthquake now.
You take on the water
and I'll supply the row."

❖ If Cupid's loving mummy
called him Eros when in Rome,
she probably regretted it
and took him straight back home.

Mythology

❖ Hercules voted Labour
   in the Tilos bi-election
   after doing twelve tremendous tasks
   in the "famous heroes" section.

❖ Helen's husband, after all,
   who, as the King of Sparta,
   when Paris had abducted her
   was fed up ever afta.

❖ Lady Bacchus was content
   to let her Lord combine
   his three well-known indulgences;
   good friends, good food, good wine.

Mythology

❖ Did Mrs. Agamemnon rise
  at 25 to 4
  and shoot her snoring husband
  after the Trojan War?

❖ With very few possessions,
  Diogenes would hate
  to move from his old barrel when
  approached by Al the Great.

Language

❖ "Abandon hope ye Latin pupils!"
   Little will excite 'em
   as long as 'number', 'case' and 'gender'
   rule ad infinitum.

❖ French teachers seem to me to have
   designs upon your jugular
   by giving you those awful verbs,
   so odd and so irregular.

❖ Taking Spanish lessons can
   be fun for all the papas
   especially when they learn to order
   lots of tasty tapas.

Language

❖ French as "she" is spoken
  in downtown Montreal
  doesn't sound how I had learned
  it years ago at all …

❖ Mandarin may be the next
  important tongue to learn
  considering China's influence
  at every trading turn.

❖ German students often wish
  the words were a little shorter.
  It's not easy writing
  Schwarzwälderkirchetorte.

Drama

❖ Freddy and Eliza
 went waltzing gaily on
 through each 3rd act performance
 of Shaw's Pygmalion.

Drama

❖ Mrs. Bizet found it just
  a little bit alarmin'
  when Georges became infatuated
  with the charmin' Carmen.

❖ Senora Verdi passed the time
  (she was an avid reader),
  with any little novelette
  while Giuseppe wrote Aida.

❖ Pygmalion, a canny King,
  had made a figurine
  who then became his blushing bride,
  his well-belovèd Queen.

Drama

❖ Desdemona's worried stiff
  at facing an embargo.
  She tried to claim that she'll refrain
  from trusting that Iago.

❖ Mimi wasn't married but
  we think she'd like to be
  when they crawl about in the dark,
  searching for her key.
  Her hands are rather chilly
  and she has a nasty cough
  and at the end of La Bohème,
  we know the wedding's off.

❖ Operatic characters
  are sometimes not related
  but the story-line is often just
  a little complicated!

Drama

❖ The strangest bits of theatre
I think I ever heard,
in la Bohème, to me were both
dramatic'ly absurd.
The young musician said the parsley
killed the pesky parrot
and Mimi sang herself to death
in the chilly Paris garret.

English Language

❖ Perhaps an oxymoron, like
  a factual form of fiction
  could be considered an example
  of a contradiction.

❖ I don't find it difficult
  or an imposition
  avoiding ending sentences
  with a puny preposition.

❖ Mistaken for a mission'ry
  whose humour wasn't huge,
  Miss Anne Thropy resembled
  crabby Ebenezer Scrooge.

English Language

***

❖ No matter how the eulogy
of honour might appear,
it always sounds a little like
an onomatopoeia.

❖ To pop the question men take
an undignified position,
ending the nervous sentence
with a bent-knee proposition.

❖ If I'm accused of being
an inveterate noun-dropper,
at least collectively uncommon,
they're never quite improper.

English Language

❖ Call me pedantic if you like
  but I must admit
  I hate to see infinitives
  unmercifully split.

❖ Departing from the singular
  can cause all sorts of trouble
  if you express a negative
  dialectically double.

❖ The adjectives a good old college
  friend of mine preferred
  were elegant examples
  with the epithets transferred.

English Language

❖ Anyone who undertakes
   exaggeration verbally
   may be accused of using some
   extreme hyperbole.

❖ With adjectives describing nouns,
   between them and betwixt,
   similarly, metaphors
   may be a little mixed.

❖ An aphorism is a maxim,
   both pithy and quite short
   but it doesn't necessarily
   expect a quick retort.

❖ Referring to the soldier's faults
   and doubtful relative,
   the sergeant used a rather nasty
   double negative.

English Literature

❖ There never was a Mrs. Crusoe
or an apple pie day,
however all domestic chores
were always done by Friday.

English Literature

❖ Having so many children,
all she had to do
was apply to social welfare
for a bigger blinkin' shoe.

❖ Mrs. Dickens hoped he'd had
some very rich relations
who'd make a will, thus leaving Charles
with some great expectations.

❖ Mrs. Chaucer said she wouldn't
visit darkest Wales,
she'd rather stay with Geoff and hear
his Canterbury Tales.

English Literature

- Mrs. Fagin may have lived
  by other sorts of nicking.
  She never featured in the tale
  of Twist and pocket-picking.

- Mrs. Dickens married Charles
  when he was at his peak
  but she didn't like their residence,
  the house was rather bleak.

- Mrs. Chekov went to pick
  a basketful of berries
  but Anton re-directed her
  to an orchard full of cherries.

English Literature

- ❖ Mrs. Marlow knew the truth
  of whether Chris had written
  any of the Shakespeare plays
  with which the world was smitten.

- ❖ Mrs. Milton wondered what
  the missing toys had cost
  when searching for the pair 'o dice
  her husband said he'd lost.

- ❖ Mrs. Wittington kept a cat
  that turned again at Ealing
  long after Dick, the city's mayor,
  spoke out once more with feeling.

English Literature

❖ Mrs. Dickens was excited,
  nearly had the vapours
  at the prospect, Charles explained,
  of wealth from *Pickwick Papers.*

❖ Mrs. Tolstoy, I suppose,
  adored her famous Count
  especially when his *War and Peace*
  had earned a large amount.

❖ Was poetic licence used
  to carry out her wish
  when Mrs. Shelley told the parson,
  "Call him Percy Bysshe?"

English Literature

❖ Romeo's fear of heights had not
   perturbed him yet unduly,
   nor did it when he scaled the wall
   to meet his darling Julie.

❖ Mrs. Holmes is never mentioned
   by the great detective.
   Perhaps her part in Sherlock's life
   was somewhat ineffective.

❖ Fanny Brawne, so loved by Keats
   and sharing John's abodes,
   provides romantic interludes
   between all those great odes.

English Literature

❖ Simone de Beauvoir wasn't quite
his real next of kin
but Jean Paul Sartre invited her
to come and live in sin.

❖ Mrs. Hardy was alarmed
with nothing in the fridge
so she went shopping on the proceeds
of *The Mayor of Casterbridge*.

❖ Did a dagger make his lady
Scotland's tragic wife
the moment he became the very
dreadful Mac the Knife?

English Literature

❖ Mrs. Wordsworth liked to wander
   in the dales and hills
   where she also saw the host
   of golden daffodils.

❖ Mrs. Attenborough went to church
   at nearly 6 o'clock
   but Richard stayed down on the beach
   with a stick of Brighton rock.

❖ Mrs. Kipling never heard
   of anyone called Kim
   but Rudyard made his name, they say,
   immortalising him.

English Literature

- Mr. Cartland was embarrassed
  by his wife's addiction
  to steamy stories of the bedroom,
  popular but fiction.

- Mr. Christie set the mousetrap
  well supplied with cheese
  which gave his wife the bright idea
  to make her play a 'tease'.

- Rudyard left it to his wife
  to keep house and to cook
  while he ensured his future fame
  by writing *Jungle Book*.

English Literature

❖ Lady Byron was upset
when George made out with sis.
She didn't think it very nice
to seek such naughty bliss.

❖ Hamlet's mother may have been
the lady he loved most
but he became somewhat distraught
on seeing Daddy's ghost.

❖ Mrs. Bolingbroke was wondering
what on earth to do
when her son became that well-known
Henry, IV Pt I & II.

English Literature

❖ When Mrs. Brooke relaxed one day
   beneath the apple tree,
   her thoughts of Rupert were quite sad
   when her watch said ten to three.

English Literature

❖ Mrs. G. K. Chesterton
declared with perfect timing,
she much preferred her husband when
he gave up beer and rhyming.

❖ Mrs. Cervantes told her son,
who wore a fetching goatee,
"You'll earn your ever-lasting fame
by writing *Don Quixote*."

❖ Mrs. Foster, wife of the doctor,
also came to the puddle
but she stepped around it as soon as she
found it and gave the wet doctor a cuddle.

English Literature

❖ It took Lord Chatterley some time
completely to recover
after his nasty gamekeeper
seduced his Lady-lover.

❖ Mrs. Rattigan liked the plays
that Terence used to write
but wished he wouldn't do it
by staying up all night.

❖ Mrs. Swift's philosophy
(said Jonathon in fun)
was, "Nothing's big or small you see
but by comparison."

English Literature

❖ Mrs. Ibsen liked to swim
in the Norwegian sea
while Henrik stayed at home to write
his plays and make the tea.

❖ Mrs. Hitchcock had her doubts
about his wicked words
when Alfred spoke of scaring us
with all those flocks of birds.

❖ Mrs. Bumble never thought
her tubby hubby crass
when he uttered, "What the Dickens sir,
I s'pose the law's a hass."

English Literature

❖ Mrs. Defoe went overboard,
the first Defoe to do so
when Daniel wrote about the sailor
Robinson de Crusoe.

❖ Mrs. Stevenson's criticism
cannot be denied,
not liking Robert Louis' tale
of Jekyll and Mr. Hyde.

❖ When asked why Ern had gone to write
about the war in Spain,
Mrs. Hemingway, alas,
could never quite explain.

English Literature

❖ Mrs. J.B. Priestley
   liked the fortune John had earned
   by means of good companions
   for whom they often yearned.

❖ Known as Mrs. Orwell,
   she shed a little tear
   on finding she could never play
   the games on Wigan Pier.

❖ Minnie Mouse, presumably,
   was quite a close relation
   who loved the way that Mickey coped
   with ev'ry situation.

English Literature

❖ Mrs. Ogden Nash explained,
"This is the silly season
when my old man decides its time
to write some rhyme and reason."

❖ Mrs. Galsworthy never offered
John a glass of lager
when he was so preoccupied
with the Forsytes and their saga.

❖ Mrs. Dante thought she knew
her Alighieri well
until he wrote his masterpiece
about a glimpse of Hell.

English Literature

❖ They say (about Caligula)
  he idolised his horse.
  In coming to a sticky end,
  he bit the dust of course.

❖ Mrs. Falstaff managed to
  adopt a hidden profile.
  Jack never would reveal her name
  'till he was very senile.

❖ Mr. Plath (American),
  but one of the better kind,
  would surely have been most upset
  at Silvia's state of mind.

English Literature

❖ Mrs. Eliot may have worn
a dozen different hats
but none delighted T.S. more
than 'Keeper of the Cats'.

English Literature

❖ Mrs. Pasternak deplored
Joe's cultural embargo
but Boris hit the jackpot with
his doctorate, "Zhivago."

❖ Was there a Mrs. Conrad
and did she cook for him?
Did she proof-read Joseph's novels?
Did she like Lord Jim?

❖ The moral of the story:
when a contract has been made,
Like Hamelin's Pied Piper,
you're entitled to be paid.